SELINA "CAT" KYLE

Selina Kyle is a teenage orphan who witnessed the murder of Bruce Wayne's parents. A street thief and skilled pickpocket, she becomes Fish Mooney's assistant during a gang war with mob boss Sal Maroni.

CARMINE FALCONE

Carmine Falcone is the head of Gotham City's largest organized crime network. Highly influential in the government and police department, Falcone also controls other gang leaders such as Fish Mooney and Oswald Cobblepot. Following the death of Sal Maroni, Falcone retired from his life of crime, telling Detective Jim Gordon that it was time for the law to save Gotham.

EDWARD NYGMA

Edward Nygma works as a forensic scientist for the Gotham City Police Department. Clever and egotistical, he is fascinated by riddles and clues. Due to his hopeless infatuation with department archivist Kristen Kringle, Nygma kills her abusive boyfriend, beginning his slide into a dark mental psychosis.

FISH MOONEY

Maria Mercedes Mooney, otherwise known as "Fish," was a sadistic gang leader and nightclub owner who stopped at nothing in her quest for power. At the end of the Gotham gang war, she murdered rival crime boss Sal Maroni and attempted to kill Carmine Falcone before being shoved off a building by Oswald Cobblepot.

GOTHAM'S ROGUES GALLERY

OSWALD COBBLEPOT – THE PENGUIN

Oswald Cobblepot aka the Penguin has the brains of a chess grandmaster and the morals of a jackal. Once the low-level umbrella man for gangster Fish Mooney and the manager of the Falcone crime family's nightclub, he hides a sadistic lust for power behind an exquisitely polite demeanor.

PROPERTY OF:

_____

INSIGHTS

INSIGHT EDITIONS

San Rafael, California
www.insighteditions.com
INED36525